Heart Mysteries

50
Poems from
Ireland to
Touch the Soul

ABOUT THE AUTHOR

Marie Heaney was born in County Tyrone and is married with three children. She is the editor of *Sources* and *Sunday Miscellany*, also published by TownHouse. She has also written two books of Irish legends, *Over Nine Waves* (Faber and Faber, 1994) and *Names Upon the Harp* (Faber and Faber, 2000).

Heart Mysteries

50
Poems from Ireland to Touch the Soul

Selected and Introduced by
MARIE HEANEY

First published in 2003 by

TownHouse, Dublin
THCH Ltd
Trinity House
Charleston Road
Ranelagh
Dublin 6
Ireland

© introduction and text introducing poems, Marie Heaney, 2003
© poems, individual copyright holders, see page 138

The title *Heart Mysteries* comes from WB Yeats' poem
'The Circus Animals' Desertion'.

1 2 3 4 5 6 7 8 9 10

ISBN: 1-86059-192-2

Cover design by Fiona Andreanelli
Text design and typeset by Fiona Andreanelli
Motifs supplied by Dover Publications
Printed by CPI Bath

CONTENTS

INTRODUCTION

The poems I have chosen for this collection deal with love and loss, two of the most powerful emotions we can experience. The themes have been broadly interpreted and the material in the book covers a wide emotional spectrum: affection, sexual longing, familial ties, grief, separation and disappointment all find expression in these pages. The love of familiar places is here too, and the sadness of emigration; the uncertainty of love alongside the rapture; anger as well as loss; and poems about those fundamentals of our existence, birth and death.

Poetry is, of its nature, a concentrated form of writing, using allusion and metaphor for effect. The personal and sometimes oblique vision that poets bring to their work is what gives it its power and individuality, but this intense focus can sometimes present difficulties for the reader. For that reason, I have chosen poems from the work of each of the poets that I felt could be called 'accessible'. However, I have chosen each poem because I believe it to be a good poem, rather than just an accessible one.

Within the limits imposed by the chosen themes and the prerequisite that the poems come from Ireland, I have aimed for as much diversity as possible. Some poems will be familiar to some readers, others will be new to most. There are excerpts from well-known classics as well as folk songs; translations of poems written in the twelfth century and poems written within the last couple of years; poems that portray the varying perspectives of women and men.

The real problem in making my selection was not what poems to include but what ones to leave out. There are many, many poets whose work I enjoy and respect who have not found a place in this book, primarily for reasons of space. The fifty poems I have included are here not only because they appeal to me, but also because they interlink, in particular ways, with other poems in this anthology.

While I know that you, the readers, will bring your own sensibility and experience to bear on the poems in *Heart Mysteries*, I have written a brief note about each one highlighting what I found significant in it – sometimes supplying a biographical detail that will give the poem a context, sometimes pointing out a device or technique that the poet has used to good effect.

I hope that the poems I have chosen for this selection will touch you as they have touched me, that they will speak to you and for you, and will help you to appreciate your heart and its mysteries.

Marie Heaney
August 2003

I have chosen 'The Long Garden' to open this selection because it is one of my favourite poems. It has a special appeal for me because it relates so closely to my own experience. Like Patrick Kavanagh, I grew up in rural Ulster and, happy as my childhood was, I sometimes felt that I was suspended in a time and place that was cut off from that world 'where life can drink his fill'.

Kavanagh catches that mood perfectly. The joy of children at play radiates from the poem but there is a wistful note too. It comes from the adult's realisation that the life the children yearn for will arrive all too quickly and will bring disappointment in its wake.

THE LONG GARDEN

It was the garden of the golden apples,
A long garden between a railway and a road,
In the sow's rooting where the hen scratches
We dipped our fingers in the pockets of God.

In the thistly hedge old boots were flying sandals
By which we travelled through the childhood skies,
Old buckets rusty-holed with half-hung handles
Were drums to play when old men married wives.

The pole that lifted the clothes-line in the middle
Was the flag-pole on a prince's palace when
We looked at it through fingers crossed to riddle
In evening sunlight miracles for men.

It was the garden of the golden apples,
And when the Carrick train went by we knew
That we could never die till something happened
Like wishing for a fruit that never grew,

Or wanting to be up on Candle-Fort
Above the village with its shops and mill.
The racing cyclists' gasp-gapped reports
Hinted of pubs where life can drink his fill.

And when the sun went down into Drumcatton
And the New Moon by its little finger swung
From the telegraph wires, we knew how God had happened
And what the blackbird in the whitethorn sang.

It was the garden of the golden apples,
The half-way house where we had stopped a day
Before we took the west road to Drumcatton
Where the sun was always setting on the play.

Patrick Kavanagh (1904–1967)

In *Waiting for Godot* by Samuel Beckett, the character Pozzo says, 'They give birth astride of a grave, the light gleams an instant, then it's night once more.' In this piece, Derek Mahon has transcended Beckett's bleak image. The poem is full of poignancy, but is permeated with brightness and sweetness too.

AN IMAGE FROM BECKETT

In that instant
There was a sea, far off,
As bright as lettuce,

A northern landscape
And a huddle
Of houses along the shore.

Also, I think, a white
Flicker of gulls
And washing hung to dry —

The poignancy of those
Back yards — and the gravedigger
Putting aside his forceps.

Then the hard boards
And darkness once again.
But in that instant

I was struck by the
Sweetness and light,
The sweetness and light,

Imagining what grave
Cities, what lasting monuments,
Given the time.

They will have buried
Our great-grandchildren, and theirs,
Beside us by now

With a subliminal batsqueak
Of reflex lamentation.
Our knuckle bones

Litter the rich earth
Changing, second by second,
To civilizations.

It was good while it lasted,
And if it only lasted
The Biblical span

Required to drop six feet
Through a glitter of wintry light,
There is No One to blame.

Still, I am haunted
By that landscape,
The soft rush of its winds,

The uprightness of its
Utilities and schoolchildren —
To whom in my will,

This, I have left my will.
I hope they have time,
And light enough, to read it.

Derek Mahon (*b.*1941)

This lament for a countryside abandoned by its inhabitants sounds a note that is still relevant two hundred years after it was written. Though the reasons for today's flight from the land are different from those that Goldsmith describes, the results are sadly familiar, with the added ill that now the very birds he mentions are threatened.

from THE DESERTED VILLAGE

Along thy glades, a solitary guest,
The hollow-sounding bittern guards its nest;
Amidst thy desert walks the lapwing flies,
And tires their echoes with unvaried cries.
Sunk are thy bowers in shapeless ruin all,
And the long grass o'ertops the mould'ring wall;
And trembling, shrinking from the spoiler's hand,
Far, far away, thy children leave the land.

Ill fares the land, to hast'ning ills a prey,
Where wealth accumulates, and men decay:
Princes and lords may flourish, or may fade;
A breath can make them, as a breath has made;
But a bold peasantry, their country's pride,
When once destroy'd, can never be supplied.

Oliver Goldsmith (1728–1774)

Wordsworth called them 'spots of time' – those seemingly insignificant moments that for no apparent reason fix themselves in our memory and have a great emotional effect on us in later years. These seven lines, written over a hundred years ago, remind us of the potency of such moments.

FOUR DUCKS ON A POND

Four ducks on a pond,
A grass bank beyond,
A blue sky of spring,
White birds on the wing:
What a little thing
To remember for years—
To remember with tears!

William Allingham (1824–1889)

Celebration of the natural world and of the seasons is one of the most outstanding features of early Irish literature. Tradition has it that Finn MacCool, the legendary hero, composed a poem in praise of spring, the season he liked best, so Peter Fallon's poem is one of the latest in a tradition that stretches back over a thousand years.

SPRING SONG

It was as if
someone only had to say
Abracadabra
to set alight
the chestnut
candelabra.

Bloom and blossom
everywhere, on furze,
on Queen Anne's Lace.
A breeze blew
cherry snows
on the common place.

Weeds on walls;
the long grass
of the long acre;
the elderberry bushes
blazing thanks
to their maker.

Loud leaves of
southside trees,
the reticent buds of ash,
the reach of undergrowth
were voices, voices,
woods' panache.

Cub foxes.
Cock pheasants braced
themselves to sing.
The white thorn flowers
were the light infantry
of Spring

marching down the headlands.
A new flock flowed
through a breach,
a makeshift gate.
And this is heaven:
sunrise through a copper beech.

Peter Fallon (*b.*1951)

Nuala Ní Dhomhnaill and Medbh McGuckian are two of the most original Irish poets of their generation, writing in Irish and English respectively. Here, in their distinctive voices, they deal with what the French call a *coup de foudre* – a bolt out of the blue, a falling head over heels in love. The point of takeoff for Nuala Ní Dhomhnaill's poem is Botticelli's painting *Primavera*. Medbh McGuckian's translation, with its vibrant use of colloquial phrases, gives an Irish spin to her English-language version of the poem.

PRIMAVERA

D'athraigh gach aon ní nuair a ghaibh sí féin thar bráid.
Bhainfeadh sí deora áthais as na clocha glasa, deirim leat.
Na héanlaithe beaga a bhí go dtí seo faoi smál,
d'osclaíodar a scornach is thosnaigh ag píopáil
ar chuma feadóige stáin i láimh gheocaigh, amhail
is gur chuma leo sa diabhal an raibh nó nach raibh nóta acu.
Bláthanna fiaine a bhí chomh cúthail, chomh humhal
ag lorg bheith istigh go faichilleach ar chiumhaiseanna
na gceapach mbláth, táid anois go rábach, féach an falcaire fiain
ag baint radharc na súl díom go hobann lena réiltíní craorag.

Bhíos-sa, leis, ag caoi go ciúin ar ghéag,
i bhfolach faoi dhuilleog fige, éalaithe i mo dhú dara,
ag cur suas stailce, púic orm chun an tsaoil.
Thógfadh sé i bhfad níos mó ná meangadh gáire
ó aon spéirbhean chun mé a mhealladh as mo shliogán,
bhí an méid sin fógartha thall is abhus agam roimh ré.
Ach do dhein sí é, le haon searradh amháin dá taobh,
le haon sméideadh meidhreach, caithiseach, thar a gualainn
do chorraigh sí na rútaí ionam, is d'fhág mé le míobhán
im' cheann, gan cos ná láimh fúm, ach mé corrathónach,
    guagach.

Nuala Ní Dhomhnaill (b.1952)

PRIMAVERA

Her ladyship hitting the scene
has fairly banjaxed me —
I swear, she'd split the sides laughing
of the dourest oul' stone.

The weeest birds that had to toe the line
have all got a licence to sing their hearts out;
like a fourteen-year-old with a tinwhistle
they couldn't care less if they haven't a note
between them.

The wild flowers that butter wouldn't melt
in their mouth, hanging around
the borders, have taken over the beds;
there's the pimpernel, knocking the eye
from my head with its ruddy fireworks.

I wasn't at myself at all, feeling out
of it, my bushel under a fig-leaf,
down in the dumps, a chip on my shoulder,
fed up to the teeth.

And the world and its granny knew
it would take a damn sight more
than a sexy smile from a bit of stuff
to get my defences down.

But she did the trick; with a single squirl
and one casual, suggestive sideglance,
she wiped the floor with me, took the feet
from under me, put my wits astray
till I'm stuck wide-eyed and legless.

translated from the Irish by Medbh McGuckian (b.1950)

This is Desmond O'Grady's sparkling translation of a poem by Antoine Raftery, a folk poet and fiddler who was born in 1774. It is a love poem to Mary Egan (the more common translation is Mary Hynes), a local beauty who captivated Raftery. One of the ironies of the poem is that Raftery, who was blind, never saw the beauty he praises so eloquently.

Yeats, who owned a tower in Bally-na-Lee, celebrated the mythologising effect of Raftery's poem in his own poem 'The Tower'. Though nearly a century had passed since Raftery's time, Yeats met people who knew Mary and remembered: 'that if walked she there,/ Farmers jostled at the fair/ So great a glory did the song confer.'

THE LASS FROM BALLY-NA-LEE

On my way to Mass
     to say a prayer,
The wind was high
      sowing rain,
I met a maid
    with wind-wild hair
And madly fell
    in love again.
I spoke with learning,
      charm and pride
And, as was fitting,
      answered she:
'My mind is now
     well satisfied
So walk with me
    to Bally-na-Lee.'
Given the offer
    I didn't delay
And blowing a laugh
      at this willing young lass,
I swung with her over
      the fields through the day
Till shortly we reached
     the rump of the house.

A table with glasses
     and drink was set
And then says the lassie
     turning to me:
'You are welcome Raftery,
     so drink a wet
To love's demands
    in Bally-na-Lee.'

I've walked in my time
     across England and France,
From Spain to Greece
     and back by sea;
Met many a maid
    at many a dance,
But none had an airy
     grace like she.
If I had the power
    and the flower of youth,
I'd find her out
    wherever she'd be,
I'd comb all the coasts
     from Cork to Beirut,
To live with this gem
    from Bally-na-Lee.

Mary Egan
   is a bred lass,
With the looks and grace
     of the queen of a tribe;

Looks, two hundred scholars
                                    en masse,
Or the pick of the poets
                                    could never describe.
Venus and Deirdre
                        were no more grand,
Nor Helen, who launched
                                    the ships in the sea,
She's the brightest blossom
                                    of all Ireland,
This fabulous flower
                        from Bally-na-Lee.
My star of light,
                        my autumn sun,
My curly head,
                        my summer sky,
In Sunday's shadow
                        let's rise and run
And arrange the place
                        where we shall lie.
All I ask is to sing
                        to you each Sunday night,
With drink on the table
                        and you on my knee—
Dear God high in Heaven,
                        who gives and takes sight,
Allow me this pleasure
                        in Bally-na-Lee.

Antoine Raftery (c.1784–1835)
translated from the Irish by Desmond O'Grady (b.1935)

This is that rare thing – a poem that makes you laugh. But under its conversational surface there lies a good deal of irony and layer after layer of attitudes to sexual matters (we bring our own to bear on those of Auntie Gerry and her nephew). In characteristic fashion, Paul Durcan handles a thought-provoking theme lightly and with deadpan humour.

AUNTIE GERRY'S FAVOURITE MARRIED NEPHEW SEAMUS

After dropping his eldest boy back to boarding school
Seamus was driving home to Athlone with another man
When he came upon a woman hitching a lift.
He lifted her and the next thing –
She offered him sex. In the car!
Seamus was shell-shocked.
It's a miracle he didn't crash.
He was very embarrassed!
In front of the other man!
But as I said to him on the phone –
In a crisis he always phones me –
Wasn't he lucky that he wasn't alone?
That he had the other man with him?

Paul Durcan (*b.*1944)

This poem is set in California. In it, John Montague evokes wonderfully the uncertainty and doubt attendant on the early stages of a love affair. The setting is a railway station, that most transient of locations. The delayed arrival of the loved one, together with the coming and goings of long-distance trains, adds to the feeling of anxiety that is allayed, to some degree, by the circle that the old lady draws round the lovers.

ALL LEGENDARY OBSTACLES

All legendary obstacles lay between
Us, the long imaginary plain,
The monstrous ruck of mountains
And, swinging across the night,
Flooding the Sacramento, San Joaquin,
The hissing drift of winter rain.

All day I waited, shifting
Nervously from station to bar
As I saw another train sail
By, the San Francisco Chief or
Golden Gate, water dripping
From great flanged wheels.

At midnight you came, pale
Above the negro porter's lamp.
I was too blind with rain
And doubt to speak, but
Reached from the platform
Until our chilled hands met.

You had been travelling for days
With an old lady, who marked
A neat circle on the glass
With her glove, to watch us
Move into the wet darkness
Kissing, still unable to speak.

John Montague (b.1929)

Though this elegant, clever poem takes the form of a conundrum, it expresses a real dilemma, one that, from time to time, is all too familiar to people in a close relationship. The poet adds another twist to the work by the ambiguity of the title.

MOONSHINE

To think
I must be alone:
To love
We must be together.

I think I love you
When I'm alone
More than I think of you
When we're together.

I cannot think
Without loving
Or love
Without thinking.

Alone I love
To think of us together:
Together I think
I'd love to be alone.

Richard Murphy (*b.*1927)

This poem, by the Northern poet W R Rodgers, is a salutation to anger. It describes a situation that will be known to most couples, but there is an exhilaration in it that is unexpected and striking. The man, as well as the woman, is energised by the power of her rage.

THE LOVERS

After the tiff there was stiff silence, till
One word, flung in centre like single stone,
Starred and cracked the ice of her resentment
To its edge. From that stung core opened and
Poured up one outward and widening wave
Of eager and extravagant anger.

W R Rodgers (1910–1969)

The first lines of 'Holy Thursday' lull us into a false sense of security. The scene is set: a romantic one, a couple in a café lingering over a meal. Then the pain at the heart of the poem is revealed in three quiet lines. And the poem continues calmly as if nothing had occurred but, because of what we now know, the images in the final stanza (and the title – because of the biblical events associated with it) assume a sad significance.

HOLY THURSDAY

They're kindly here, to let us linger so late,
Long after the shutters are up.
A waiter glides from the kitchen with a plate
Of stew, or some thick soup,

And settles himself at the next table but one.
We know, you and I, that it's over,
That something or other has come between
Us, whatever we are, or were.

The waiter swabs his plate with bread
And drains what's left of his wine,
Then rearranges, one by one,
the knife, the fork, the spoon, the napkin,
The table itself, the chair he's simply borrowed,
And smiles, and bows to his own absence.

Paul Muldoon (*b.*1951)

This poem, a fine example of early folk poetry, was translated from the Irish by Thomas MacDonagh, one of three poets executed for their part in the Easter Rising of 1916. In it, the lover's feelings of despair find an echo in the bleak beauty of the natural world.

THE STARS STAND UP IN THE AIR

The stars stand up in the air,
The sun and the moon are gone,
The strand of its waters is bare,
And her sway is swept from the swan.

The cuckoo was calling all day,
Hid in the branches above,
How my stórín is fled away,
'Tis my grief that I gave her my love!

Anon

translated from the Irish by Thomas MacDonagh (1878–1916)

Lady Gregory would have heard 'Dónal Óg' ('Young Donal') sung in Irish on her field trips to collect folk material in the late-nineteenth and early-twentieth centuries. The original (which is still sung today) is one of the most piercing outcries of grief in the song tradition and Lady Gregory's translation is a fitting version of a great lament. Her translation retains the elaborate metaphors of the original, which build up to give the elemental simplicity of the last stanza such force.

DONALL OGE: GRIEF OF A GIRL'S HEART

O Donall Oge, if you go across the sea,
Bring myself with you and do not forget it;
And you will have a sweetheart for fair days and market days,
And the daughter of the King of Greece beside you at night.

It is late last night the dog was speaking of you;
The snipe was speaking of you in her deep marsh.
It is you are the lonely bird through the woods;
And that you may be without a mate until you find me.

You promised me, and you said a lie to me,
That you would be before me where the sheep are flocked;
I gave a whistle and three hundred cries to you,
And I found nothing there but a bleating lamb.

You promised me a thing that was hard for you,
A ship of gold under a silver mast;
Twelve towns with a market in all of them,
And a fine white court by the side of the sea.

You promised me a thing that is not possible,
That you would give me gloves of the skin of a fish;
That you would give me shoes of the skin of a bird;
And a suit of the dearest silk in Ireland.

When I go by myself to the Well of Loneliness,
I sit down and I go through my trouble;
When I see the world and do not see my boy,
He that has an amber shade in his hair.

It was on that Sunday I gave my love to you;
The Sunday that is last before Easter Sunday.
And myself on my knees reading the Passion;
And my two eyes giving love to you for ever.

My mother said to me not to be talking with you to-day,

Or tomorrow, or on Sunday;

It was a bad time she took for telling me that;

It was shutting the door after the house was robbed.

My heart is as black as the blackness of the sloe,

Or as the black coal that is on the smith's forge;

Or as the sole of a shoe left in white halls;

It was you put that darkness over my life.

You have taken the east from me; You have taken the west from me,

You have taken what is before me and what is behind me;

You have taken the moon, you have taken the sun from me,

And my fear is great that you have taken God from me!

Anon

translated from the Irish by Lady Gregory (1852–1932)

What is striking about this traditional Irish song on a famil-
iar theme is the unfamiliar note of defiance that rings out in
the last lines.

I WILL WALK WITH MY LOVE

I once loved a boy, just a bold Irish boy
who would come and would go at my request;
and this bold Irish boy was my pride and my joy
and I built him a bow'r in my breast.

But this girl who has taken my bonny, bonny boy,
let her make of him all that she can;
and whether he loves me or loves me not,
I will walk with my love now and then.

Traditional

This haunting song, on the perennial theme of the rejected lover, is one of the best known in the Irish traditional repertoire. Elements of the song, especially the first and the last verses, appear in folk songs in other traditions as well.

THE LAMBS ON THE GREEN HILLS

The lambs on the green hills they sport and they play,
And many strawberries grow round the salt sea,
And many strawberries grow round the salt sea,
And many's the ship sails the ocean.

The bride and bride's party to church they did go,
The bride she rode foremost, she made a fine show,
But I followed behind with my heart full of woe,
For she's gone to be wed to another.

The first place I saw her 'twas in the church stand,
Gold rings on her finger and her love by the hand,
Says I, 'My wee lassie, I will be the man
Although you are wed to another.'

The next place I seen her was on the way home,
I ran on before her, not knowing where to roam,
Says I, 'My wee lassie, I'll be by your side
Although you are wed to another.'

'Stop, stop,' said the groomsman, "till I speak a word,
Will you venture your life on the point of my sword?
For courting so slowly you've lost this fair maid,
So begone, for you'll never enjoy her.'

Oh, make now my grave both large, wide and deep,
And sprinkle it over with flowers so sweet,
And lay me down in it to take my last sleep,
For that's the best way to forget her.

Traditional

The plight of the unmarried mother is a theme that recurs again and again in traditional song. This one, from the north of Ireland, was collected by singer and film maker David Hammond from Hugh Quinn, a Belfast collector of traditional songs. Though the third verse appears in many other songs, the first two verses have a directness to them that is unusual and affecting.

THERE IS A BLACKBIRD

There is a blackbird on yonder tree
They say he's blind and he cannot see
But never a girl as blind as me
When that I fell into bad company.

He courted me when I was thin
He courted me and my love did win
But now that my bib is up to my chin
He passes my door and won't come in.

I wish, I wish, I wish in vain,
I wish I was a maid again.
A maid again I never will be
Till apples grow on to an ivy tree.

I wish my baby it was born
And sitting on his daddy's knee
And me poor girl to be dead and gone
With the green, green grass growing over me.

Traditional

This is a beautiful lament that the scholar, Douglas Hyde, collected, translated and published in his collection *Love Songs of Connacht* in 1893. The theme is the all too familiar one of emigration and the grief of the lover left behind. The mood changes, however, and the poem ends on an unexpectedly erotic note.

MY GRIEF ON THE SEA

My grief on the sea,
How the waves of it roll !
For they heave between me
And the love of my soul !

Abandoned, forsaken,
To grief and to care,
Will the sea ever waken
Relief from despair ?

My grief, and my trouble !
Would he and I were
In the province of Leinster,
Or county of Clare.

Were I and my darling—
Oh, heart-bitter wound !—
On board of the ship
For America bound.

On a green bed of rushes
All last night I lay,
And I flung it abroad
With the heat of the day.

And my love came behind me—
He came from the south;
His breast to my bosom,
His mouth to my mouth.

Anon
translated from the Irish by Douglas Hyde (1860–1949)

The puritanical view of sex that obsessed Irish society in relatively recent times – and gave the censors a field day – is notably absent in 'Keep to Yourself Your Kisses' ('Taisigh Agat Féin Do Phóg'), written in Irish in the early-seventeenth century. This sensual, elegant translation is by Máire Mhac an tSaoi, who is herself a poet in the Irish language.

KEEP TO YOURSELF YOUR KISSES

Keep to yourself your kisses,
      Bright teeth and parted lip,
Keep your mouth away from me,
      I have no mind for your kiss.

A kiss more sweet than honey
      From the wife of another man
Has left without taste all kisses
      That were since the world began.

Till, and please God I may—
      I see that woman again—
Her kiss being as it was—
      I ask no other till then.

Anon
translated from the Irish by Máire Mhac an tSaoi (b.1922)

Dubliner Paula Meehan uses the colloquial speech of her native city in this poem, which has an edge of menace to it in spite of its bantering tone.

WOULD YOU JUMP INTO MY GRAVE AS QUICK?

Would you jump into my grave as quick?
my granny would ask when one of us took
her chair by the fire. You, woman,
done up to the nines, red lips a come on,
your breath reeking of drink
and your black eye on my man tonight
in a Dublin bar, think
first of the steep drop, the six dark feet.

Paula Meehan (b.1955)

John Millington Synge is best known as a playwright, his masterpiece being *The Playboy of the Western World*. Though this love poem is slight in comparison to his dramatic writing, there is a sense of intimacy about it that gives it great appeal.

WITH ONE LONG KISS

With one long kiss
Were you nearby
You'd break the dismal cloud that is
On all my sky

With one long kiss
If you were near
You'd sweeten days I take amiss
When lonely here

With one long kiss
You'd make for me
A golden paradise of this
Day's beggary

J M Synge (1871–1909)

Francis Ledwidge was a nature poet from County Meath who fought in the trenches in the First World War 'neither for a principle nor a people nor a law, but for the fields along the Boyne, for the birds and the blue sky over them'. This enigmatic poem, in which he expresses a soldier's resentment, contains an uncharacteristic note of bitterness and cynicism.

Ledwidge was killed in action in 1917.

IN A CAFÉ

Kiss the maid and pass her round,
Lips like hers were made for many.
Our loves are far from us to-night,
But these red lips are sweet as any.

Let no empty glass be seen
Aloof from our good table's sparkle,
At the acme of our cheer
Here are francs to keep the circle.

They are far who miss us most—
Sip and kiss—how well we love them,
Battling through the world to keep
Their hearts at peace, their God above them.

Francis Ledwidge (1887–1917)

This poem begins as a humorous response to the travails of minding a small child who is creating chaos and it uses war terminology to create its effect. By the end of the poem, the devastation is real and the ring on the finger of the laughing soldier reminds us that he is a husband – possibly a father – as well as the tormentor we see him to be.

MINDING RUTH

for Seamus Deane

She wreaks such havoc in my library,
It will take ages to set it right—
A Visigoth in a pinafore

Who, weakening, plonks herself
On the works of Friedrich Nietzsche,
And pines for her mother.

She's been at it all morning,
Duck-arsed in my History section
Like a refugee among rubble,

Or, fled to the toilet, calling
In a panic that the seat is cold.
But now she relents under biscuits

To extemporise grace notes,
And sketch with a blue crayon
Arrow after arrow leading nowhere.

My small surprise of language,
I cherish you like an injury
And would swear by you at this moment

For your brisk chatter brings me
Chapter and verse, you restore
The city itself, novel and humming,

Which I enter as a civilian
Who plants his landscape with place-names.
They stand an instant, and fade.

Her hands sip at my cuff. She cranes,
Perturbedly, with a book held open
At plates from Warsaw in the last war.

Why is the man with the long beard
Eating his booboos? And I stare
At the old rabbi squatting in turds

Among happy soldiers who die laughing,
The young one clapping: you can see
A wedding band flash on his finger.

Aidan Carl Mathews (b.1956)

Michael Hartnett, who was born in County Limerick, wrote poems in both Irish and English. In this lovely praise poem for his daughter, the influence of early Irish poetry, in which nature plays an integral role, is clearly evident.

POEM FOR LARA, 10

An ashtree on fire
the hair of your head
coaxing larks
with your sweet voice
in the green grass,
a crowd of daisies
playing with you,
a crowd of rabbits
dancing with you,
the blackbird
with its gold bill
is a jewel for you,
the goldfinch
with its sweetness
is your music.

You are perfume,
you are honey,
a wild strawberry:
even the bees think you
a flower in the field.
Little queen of the land of books,
may you always be thus,
may you ever be free
    from sorrow-chains.

Here's my blessing for you, girl,
and it is no petty grace —
may you have the beauty of your mother's soul
    and the beauty of her face.

Michael Hartnett (1941–1999)

Mary O'Malley was born in Connemara and, having lived abroad for some years, now lives in Galway again. In this moving poem, she recalls the trauma of her first day at school and its recurring effect on her as an adult.

STARTING SCHOOL

Motherless the first day
she stood alone in the empty schoolyard,
too early for fear of being late.
She stared and shrank
like a startled iris
as the sky exploded.

If she had given in and cried,
lain down on that grey rock
between the speckled cliff
and the humpy hill
she might have cried it out,
but the eldest must be strong.

Now, glancing through the kitchen window
or during a summer walk
a certain texture of stone
with no give in it drives her out
into the raw tundra of dreams.
At the edge of the horizon
between the hill and the speckled cliff
a dry-eyed child sits, frozen.

Mary O'Malley (b.1954)

This is another poem that reminds us how, unexpectedly, an everyday occurrence can achieve great significance and lodge itself in the memory. In this case, the poet's sudden sense of abandonment as a child resurfaces as grief after the death of his father and as guilt when, now a father himself, he sees the wheel come full circle.

LESSER DEATHS

for Josie

**So it's farewell to Ballybunion,
Will I ever see thee more?**

A memory lingers without evident point
Of my father one ordinary morning
Conveying me the road to school
As far as the turn, to check the cows were
Safely grazing in the right field,
Shepherded by the steady pulse
Of the electric fence, and then
Turning back as I walked on. Once
I turned to see his back steadily
Walking from me and was pierced
By a knife which twisted years after
When his heart stopped beating. Now,
Josie, sand-absorbed, hands me a spade,
Laughing, chattering: then slams thumb
In mouth with a silent stare when I say
I must leave her and go to work.

Bernard O'Donoghue (*b.*1945)

Eavan Boland's interest in the place of women in mythology and legend has inspired a number of her poems. In this poem to her daughter, she celebrates the eternal and consoling nature of legend itself as it is re-lived generation by generation.

LEGENDS

for Eavan Frances

Tryers of firesides,
twilights. There are no tears in these.

Instead, they begin the world again,
making the mountain ridges blue
and the rivers clear and the hero fearless —

and the outcome always undecided
so the next teller can say *begin* and
again and astonish children.

Our children are our legends.
You are mine. You have my name.
My hair was once like yours.

And the world
is less bitter to me
because you will re-tell the story.

Eavan Boland (*b.*1944)

Letters from young Irish emigrants to the parents they have left behind were a feature of poems and ballads in the nineteenth and early-twentieth centuries. In this poem, written at the end of the twentieth century, Tom Paulin gives the genre a new twist.

TRACES

They are so light,
Those airmail letters.
Their blueness has fallen
From an Indian sky,
The hot taut atmosphere
Above the muddled village
Your parents write from.

'With God's help,
The crops have been brought
Safely in. All here
Are well, ten *lakhs* of rupees
Our lands are worth now.
That boy's father has twenty acres.
The buffalo are fine,
Though the heat is hard to bear.'

All the fierce passions
Of family and property
Are dictated to a scribe
Who understands English,
Has a daughter to marry
And a dusty handful
Of aluminium coins.

Tom Paulin (*b.*1949)

In 'Oranges', the poet looks lovingly in at her family living their own lives and captures the moment for us with photographic clarity. Her outsider status enables her to see her family's happiness and to celebrate it, but it also brings with it a rueful sense of her own dispensability.

Vona Groarke was brought up in Lissoy, County Westmeath, 'two fields away' from the parsonage in which Oliver Goldsmith spent his childhood.

ORANGES

Say you approach   your house in winter
home from work   or in from the shops.
The light is on   in your living room
and the blind   still up. So you stop
to watch the shape   your family makes
against your home.   Your lover reaches
to a high shelf.   He could see you
if he turned his   head your way.
Your daughter   reads some words
you did not write.   Your son juggles
two oranges   or is in flight
between corners   of the room.
Your life shines   without you.
The keys blaze   in your palm.

Vona Groarke (b.1964)

Thomas Kinsella is one of Ireland's foremost poets and translators. This translation of a seventeenth-century love poem delights as much in the lushness and freshness of nature as it does in the beauty and appeal of the woman to whom it is addressed.

SHE'S THE BLACKBERRY-FLOWER

She's the blackberry-flower,
the fine raspberry-flower,
she's the plant of best breeding
        your eyes could behold:
she's my darling and dear,
my fresh apple-tree flower,
she is Summer in the cold
        between Christmas and Easter.

Anon

translated from the Irish by Thomas Kinsella (b.1928)

This memorable love poem is by Austin Clarke, one of the most important writers of twentieth-century Ireland.

It is addressed to the daughter of the Big House and describes the effect the girl's legendary beauty has on those who see her. It has some of the strangeness of early Irish love poetry about it as well as a faint, but haunting, sense of unattainable love.

THE PLANTER'S DAUGHTER

When night stirred at sea
And the fire brought a crowd in,
They say that her beauty
Was music in mouth
And few in the candlelight
Thought her too proud,
For the house of the planter
Is known by the trees.

Men that had seen her
Drank deep and were silent,
The women were speaking
Wherever she went—
As a bell that is rung
Or a wonder told shyly
And O she was the Sunday
In every week.

Austin Clarke (1896–1974)

This searing outpouring of grief for his dead wife was composed around AD 1200 by Muireadach Ó Dálaigh (Murrough O'Daly). It is an early example of the great tradition of lament (or 'keen') in Gaelic poetry. The metaphors drawn from the world of nature illuminate the writing like ornamental scrollwork and are a feature of Irish poetry that persists to the present day. This powerful translation is by the celebrated writer, Frank O'Connor.

ON THE DEATH OF HIS WIFE

I parted from my life last night,
        A woman's body sunk in clay:
The tender bosom that I loved
        Wrapped in a sheet they took away.

The heavy blossom that had lit
        The ancient boughs is tossed and blown;
Hers was the burden of delight
        That long had weighed the old tree down.

And I am left alone tonight
        And desolate is the world I see
For lovely was that woman's weight
        That even last night had lain on me.

Weeping I look upon the place
        Where she used to rest her head—
For yesterday her body's length
        Reposed upon you too, my bed.

Yesterday that smiling face
        Upon one side of you was laid
That could match the hazel bloom
        In its dark delicate sweet shade.

Maelva of the shadowy brows
        Was the mead-cask at my side;
Fairest of all flowers that grow
        Was the beauty that has died.

My body's self deserts me now,
        The half of me that was her own,
Since all I knew of brightness died
        Half of me lingers, half is gone.

The face that was like hawthorn bloom
        Was my right foot and my right side;
And my right hand and my right eye
        Were no more mine than hers who died.

Poor is the share of me that's left
        Since half of me died with my wife;
I shudder at the words I speak;
        Dear God, that girl was half my life.

And our first look was her first love;
>> No man had fondled ere I came
The little breasts so small and firm
>> And the long body like a flame.

For twenty years we shared a home,
>> Our converse milder with each year;
Eleven children in its time
>> Did that tall stately body bear.

It was the King of hosts and roads
>> Who snatched her from me in her prime:
Little she wished to leave alone
>> The man she loved before her time.

Now King of churches and of bells,
>> Though never raised to pledge a lie
That woman's hand —can it be true?—
>> No more beneath my head will lie.

Muireadach Ó Dálaigh (c.1200)

translated from the Irish by Frank O'Connor (1903–1966)

There is a tradition among some members of the Irish Traveller community to burn the trailer and possessions of a family member who has died. This striking poem by Donegal poet Moya Cannon, reminds us of the grief a family endures after the death of the mother, a grief exacerbated by the marginalisation that Traveller families experience wherever they go.

AFTER THE BURIAL

They straightened the blankets,
piled her clothes onto the bed,
soaked them with petrol,
then emptied the gallon can
over the video and tape recorder,
stepped outside their trailer,
lit it, watched until only the burnt chassis was left,
gathered themselves
and pulled out of Galway.

Camped for a week in Shepherd's Bush,
then behind a glass building in Brixton,
he went into drunken mourning for his dead wife,
while their children hung around the vans,
or foraged in the long North London streets
among other children, some of whom also perhaps
    understood,
that beyond respectability's pale,
where reason and civility show their second face,
it's hard to lay ghosts.

Moya Cannon (b.1956)

'The Ballad of Reading Gaol' is a long, impassioned poem by Oscar Wilde. In this well-known extract, Wilde has just learnt that the man in the exercise yard is to be hanged for murdering his wife. Wilde, who had been a prisoner in the jail himself, is moved to write this protest poem, giving it popular appeal by using the language and metre of the ballad.

from THE BALLAD OF READING GAOL

I only knew what hunted thought
       Quickened his step, and why
He looked upon the garish day
       With such a wistful eye;
The man had killed the thing he loved,
       And so he had to die.

Yet each man kills the thing he loves,
       By each let this be heard,
Some do it with a bitter look,
       Some with a flattering word,
The coward does it with a kiss,
       The brave man with a sword!

Some kill their love when they are young,
          And some when they are old;
Some strangle with the hands of Lust,
          Some with the hands of Gold:
The kindest use a knife, because
          The dead so soon grow cold.

Some love too little, some too long,
          Some sell, and others buy;
Some do the deed with many tears,
          And some without a sigh:
For each man kills the thing he loves,
          Yet each man does not die.

Oscar Wilde (1854–1900)

James Simmons was a singer and songwriter as well as a poet. He wrote this pensive poem in the 1970s when the Troubles in his native Northern Ireland were at their height. It salutes the work of Thomas Moore, the eighteenth-century poet and songwriter, who, like Simmons, lived through a period of rebellion and political upheaval in Ireland.

FOR THOMAS MOORE

When the young have grown tired
and the old are abused,
when beauty's degraded
and brilliance not used,
when courage is clumsy
and strength misapplied
we wish that our seed
in the dark womb had died.

But when youth finds its singers
and old men find peace
and beauty finds servants
and genius release,
when courage has wisdom
and strength mends our wrongs
we will sing unembarrassed
your marvellous songs.

James Simmons (1933–2001)

Thomas Moore, who was born in Dublin, brought Irish songs into the fashionable drawing rooms of London. Some of them, lamenting the plight of his homeland, had political intent but others, like this one addressed to his wife, were more personal. Moore had a most successful professional life, but his family life was marked by tragedy and he was predeceased by all of his five children.

LOVE THEE, DEAREST? LOVE THEE?

Love thee, dearest? love thee?
      Yes, by yonder star I swear,
Which through tears above thee
      Shines so sadly fair;
Though often dim,
With tears, like him,
Like him my truth will shine,
      And — love thee, dearest? love thee?
Yes, till death I'm thine.

Leave thee, dearest? leave thee?
      No, that star is not more true;
When my vows deceive thee,
      He will wander too.
A cloud of night
May veil his light,
And death shall darken mine —
      But — leave thee, dearest? leave thee?
No, till death I'm thine.

Thomas Moore (1779–1852)

John Hewitt, usually an emotionally reserved poet, wrote this unexpectedly tender poem for his wife after observing her working in her garden. She is rejuvenated and happy and her husband rejoices in it but he notices that she has no song to express that happiness. This love poem does it for her.

FOR ROBERTA IN THE GARDEN

I know when you are at your happiest,
kneeling on mould, a trowel in your glove;
you raise your eyes and for a moment rest;
you turn a young-girl's face, like one in love.

Intent, entranced, this hour, in gardening,
surely to life's bright process you belong.
I wonder, when you pause, you do not sing,
for such a moment surely has its song.

John Hewitt (1907–1987)

This poem is haunted by the spectre of mortality and by the powerlessness of love in the face of it. As so often happens at significant moments, insignificant details are registered with great clarity and this adds to the sense of foreboding and vulnerability that permeates the poem.

Kerry Hardie was born in Singapore, brought up in County Down and now lives in Kilkenny.

THE HUSBAND'S TALE

What is a wife?
          She sits in the car and waits
while he opens the gates, the roses on the wall
all blown in the rain which is fine and warm
and just greys the green of high summer
like the fine strands now muting her hair.
She will drive to the small country town
and park in the station yard
and stand at the grooved wooden window
and take the ticket and wait in the rain for the train
to Dublin, to the doctor...
          And he thinks
how frail she is in her beige mac
in the green stew of roses and rain and birdsong,
how tired and quiet before the journey.
And he, in his strength, falters.
          A loved wife is an underbelly
as soft and as stretched for the knife
as a frog's.

Kerry Hardie (*b.*1951)

Patrick Kavanagh's poems about his mother are probably better known, but this one written about his father is simple and moving. That the poet remembers his father ill and debilitated, rather than in his prime, intensifies the feeling of sadness in the poem.

MEMORY OF MY FATHER

Every old man I see
Reminds me of my father
When he had fallen in love with death
One time when sheaves were gathered.

That man I saw in Gardner Street
Stumble on the kerb was one,
He stared at me half-eyed,
I might have been his son.

And I remember the musician
Faltering over his fiddle
In Bayswater, London,
He too set me the riddle.

Every old man I see
In October-coloured weather
Seems to say to me:
'I was once your father.'

Patrick Kavanagh (1904–1967)

Julie O'Callaghan is an American who has lived in Ireland for many years. The deal in the title is the one the poet's father made in the last year of his life as he decides to live to the full every moment that is left to him. The tough-minded sales talk of the poem's surface cannot disguise (indeed it intensifies) the grief that lies beneath.

THE DEAL

It cost everything
but he bought a year.
And once it was his
he owned the sky,
a couple of volcanoes
and every molecule
in the universe.
He figured it was pricey
but hey — it was all his.
Minutes and quarter hours
were his as far
as the eye could see.
As for months, twelve big ones
all in a row.
By the time his.
daily desk diary
was down to two pages
he had hammered out
a rock-solid deal
on what was to follow.

Julie O'Callaghan (*b.*1954)

When Louis MacNeice was five, his mother, suffering from severe depression, was hospitalised. As she left home, Louis, the youngest, and his two siblings waved to her from the garden. They never saw her again.

This poem, written when the poet was in his thirties, conveys the desolation experienced by the child. The simple vocabulary and the echoes of the nursery rhyme in the poem give it added poignancy.

AUTOBIOGRAPHY

In my childhood trees were green
And there was plenty to be seen.

Come back early or never come.

My father made the walls resound,
He wore his collar the wrong way round.

Come back early or never come.

My mother wore a yellow dress;
Gently, gently, gentleness.

Come back early or never come.

When I was five the black dreams came;
Nothing after was quite the same.

Come back early or never come.

The dark was talking to the dead;
The lamp was dark beside my bed.

Come back early or never come.

When I woke they did not care;
Nobody, nobody was there.

Come back early or never come.

When my silent terror cried,
Nobody, nobody replied.

Come back early or never come.

I got up; the chilly sun
Saw me walk away alone.

Come back early or never come.

Louis MacNeice (1907–1963)

The effect of the early death of the poet's mother on her family is what Dennis O'Driscoll investigates in this poem. The quizzical tone he uses and his litany of apparently inconsequential losses seem to underplay the significance of her death, but they are poetic red herrings. The poem opens with a matter-of-fact 'And yet' but, by the time we have read the phrase for the last time, we know how grievous the loss has been.

YEARS AFTER

And yet we managed fine.

We missed your baking for a time.
And yet were we not better off
without cream-hearted sponge cakes,
flaky, rhubarb-oozing pies?

Linoleum-tiled rooms could no longer
presume on your thoroughgoing scrub;
and yet we made up for our neglect,
laid hardwood timber floors.

Windows shimmered less often.
And yet we got around to
elbow-greasing them eventually.
Your daily sheet-and-blanket

rituals of bedmaking were more
than we could hope to emulate.
And yet the duvets we bought
brought us gradually to sleep.

Declan and Eithne (eleven
and nine respectively at the time)
had to survive without your packed
banana sandwiches, wooden spoon

deterrent, hugs, multivitamins.
And yet they both grew strong:
you have unmet grandchildren,
in-laws you never knew.

Yes, we managed fine, made
breakfasts and made love,
took on jobs and mortgages,
set ourselves up for life.

And yet. And yet. And yet.

Dennis O'Driscoll (b.1954)

'Father' manifests the powerful influence the present brings to bear on the past. And vice versa. While there is mutual betrayal in this poem, and good memories are swamped by bad, in the last line the ambivalence and guilt of a difficult relationship dissolve into love.

FATHER

Today the memories are bad.
Not the sprightly whistling man
making a daughter smile, tricks
up your sleeve, winks and gibes,

natty in trousers kept creased
under the mattress, shoes gleamed
with army spit and shine. No, today
you are the man whose polished toe

pushes away a child
crying to be lifted
to the sky between your hands,
heat of your breath on her cheeks.

And when no drinks no friends left,
don't leave me you say. But I do just that.
I walk out on you. Now I would break down doors
for one look of your face.

Sheila O'Hagan

This early poem by Seamus Heaney describes his return from boarding school to attend the funeral of a younger brother. The scene is observed with cinematic accuracy and events are reported in an unflinching way as the poem builds up to the tragic revelations contained in the last two stanzas and the finality of the last line.

MID-TERM BREAK

I sat all morning in the college sick bay
Counting bells knelling classes to a close.
At two o'clock our neighbours drove me home.

In the porch I met my father crying—
He had always taken funerals in his stride—
And Big Jim Evans saying it was a hard blow.

The baby cooed and laughed and rocked the pram
When I came in, and I was embarrassed
By old men standing up to shake my hand

And tell me they were 'sorry for my trouble'.
Whispers informed strangers I was the eldest,
Away at school, as my mother held my hand

In hers and coughed out angry tearless sighs.
At ten o'clock the ambulance arrived
With the corpse, stanched and bandaged by the nurses.

Next morning I went up into the room. Snowdrops
And candles soothed the bedside; I saw him
For the first time in six weeks. Paler now,

Wearing a poppy bruise on his left temple,
He lay in the four foot box as in his cot.
No gaudy scars, the bumper knocked him clear.

A four foot box, a foot for every year.

Seamus Heaney (b.1939)

On 31 August 1994, after more than thirty years of conflict in Northern Ireland, the IRA announced a permanent ceasefire. Frank Ormsby's poem, written shortly before that announcement was made, celebrates the birth of his daughter and discovers that true peace lies within what Thomas Moore calls 'love's shining circle'.

HELEN

b. 12 August 1994

The war will soon be over, or so they say.
Five floors below the Friday rush-hour starts.
You're out and breathing. We smile to hear you cry.
Your long fingers curl around our hearts.

The place knows nothing of you and is home.
Indifferent skies look on while August warms
the middle air. We wrap you in your name.
Peace is the way you settle in our arms.

Frank Ormsby (*b.*1947)

This poem is set during the Siege of Troy. The Greek hero Achilles has just killed Hector, son of Priam, the king of Troy. Priam wants to give his son an honourable burial and, slipping out of his besieged city, goes to Achilles' tent and kisses the hand of his enemy. The Greek hero takes pity on the defenceless king and gives him his son's body. He also concedes to Priam's request that there be a ceasefire while the Trojans mourn Hector and prepare a hero's funeral for him. So there are eleven days of cessation of violence within the long and bloody war.

The poem retains all the classical elements of the original story, but there is a correlation between the events in ancient Troy and those in Longley's native Northern Ireland.

CEASEFIRE

I

Put in mind of his own father and moved to tears
Achilles took him by the hand and pushed the old king
Gently away, but Priam curled up at his feet and
Wept with him until their sadness filled the building.

II

Taking Hector's corpse into his own hands Achilles
Made sure it was washed and, for the old king's sake,
Laid out in uniform, ready for Priam to carry
Wrapped like a present home to Troy at daybreak.

III

When they had eaten together, it pleased them both
To stare at each other's beauty as lovers might,
Achilles built like a god, Priam good-looking still
And full of conversation, who earlier had sighed:

IV

'I get down on my knees and do what must be done
And kiss Achilles' hand, the killer of my son.'

Michael Longley (*b*.1939)

The summer of 1998 was a hopeful time in Northern Ireland, a time when a peaceful, normal life seemed a possibility. Those hopes were blown apart on Saturday, 15 August 1998 in Omagh, County Tyrone, when a bomb exploded killing 29 men, women and children. This poem describes the desolation in the town in the aftermath of the explosion and makes a powerful, if almost despairing, plea for peace.

SUNDAY, 16 AUGUST 1998

In Omagh
on a deserted street just after dawn
there was no one abroad
but some lone cameraman

taking a shot for the news. And at a slight incline
above the piled debris
the only thing still working
beyond his lens

was the traffic lights.
And there, though no car stirred,
the lights went red,
the lights went green,

and red, and green again;
for Stop, though no one stopped,
for Go, though no one went,
nor stopped, nor went again.

Undisturbed by all that happened
the lights still kept urging traffic
through the crack that opened
between ten-after-three

and eternity. And then they went faster
as if the bomb had damaged time itself,
then slowed again as if somehow they could
go back to normality.

Then faster still, the light for Stop,
the light for Go, the light for Stop,
the light for Go, the light for Stop,

for Stop, for Stop, for Stop.

Dermot Healy (b.1947)

'Taking a last look' was a phrase that country people used if they saw an old or ailing person move around looking long at familiar scenes. There is such a strong sense of imminent death – of a last look – in this poem that it feels like an elegy.

THAT SUMMER

So what did she do that summer
When they were all out working?

If she moved she felt a soft rattle
That settled like a purseful of small change.
She staggered through the quiet of the house,
Leaned on a flowering doorpost
And went back inside from the glare
Feeling in her skirt pocket the skin on her hands,
Never so smooth since her fourteenth year.

One warm evening they were late;
She walked across the yard with a can,
Watered a geranium and kept on going
Till she came to the ridge looking over the valley
At the low stacked hills, the steep ground
Between that plunged like a funnel of sand.
She couldn't face back home, they came for her
As she stood watching the hills breathing out and in,
Their dialogue of hither and yon.

Eiléan Ní Chuilleanáin (b. 1942)

Katharine Tynan, who was born in County Dublin, is probably best remembered for her poem 'Sheep and Lambs' which has become famous as the choral piece 'All in the April Evening'.

This poem, with its note of peaceful acceptance, feels as if might have been written by the poet towards the end of her life. In fact, she was under thirty when she wrote it, an unhappy love affair, real or imagined, making her sound older and wiser than her years.

STORM-GOLD

After the rainy day,
>> After the stormy weather,
Breaks the gold in the grey,
>> Gold and silver together.
Flutters and falls the splendour,
>> Turns to scarlet and rose;
Clear in a sky that is tender
>> A crescent-moon grows.

After the rainy day
>> The passion and sobbing are over;
Dim in distance away
>> Seem my love and my lover.
The gold of the evening is round me,
>> Night comes with the wings of a dove;
The peace of the evening hath bound me
>> Far sweeter than love.

Katharine Tynan (1861–1931)

This poem was written in 1938 when there was political turmoil in Europe. The poet's attention is drawn away from these ominous politics, and from the alarm of the men who talk about them, to rest achingly on a young girl whose beauty reminds him of his lost youth and of the potency of sexual desire.

This poem was among the last poems that Yeats wrote before his death in January 1939.

POLITICS

How can I, that girl standing there,
My attention fix
On Roman or on Russian
Or on Spanish politics,
Yet here's a travelled man that knows
What he talks about,
And there's a politician
That has both read and thought,
And maybe what they say is true
Of war and war's alarms,
But O that I were young again
And held her in my arms.

W B Yeats (1865–1939)

PERMISSION ACKNOWLEDGEMENTS

The publisher has endeavoured to contact all copyright holders. If any errors have inadvertently been made, corrections will be made in future editions.

Eavan Boland 'Legends' from *Collected Poems* reprinted by kind permission of Carcanet Press Ltd (1995) · Moya Cannon 'After the Burial' by kind permission of the author and The Gallery Press, Loughcrew, Oldcastle, County Meath, Ireland from *Oar* (2000) · Austin Clarke 'The Planter's Daughter' reprinted by kind permission of R Dardis Clarke 17 Oscar Square, Dublin 8 · 'Auntie Gerry's Favourite Married Nephew Seamus' from *Cries of an Irish Caveman* by Paul Durcan published by The Harvill Press. Used by permission of The Random House Group Limited · Peter Fallon 'Spring Song' by kind permission of the author and The Gallery Press, Loughcrew, Oldcastle, County Meath, Ireland from *News of the World (Selected and New Poems)* (1998) · Vona Groarke 'Oranges' by kind permission of the author and The Gallery Press, Loughcrew, Oldcastle, County Meath, Ireland from *Flight* (2002) · Kerry Hardie 'The Husband's Tale' by kind permission of the author and The Gallery Press, Loughcrew, Oldcastle, County Meath, Ireland from *A Furious Place* (1996) · Michael Hartnett 'Poem for Lara, 10' by kind permission of the author and The Gallery Press, Loughcrew, Oldcastle, County Meath, Ireland from *Selected and New Poems* (1994) · Dermot Healy 'Sunday, 16 August 1998' by kind permission of the author and The Gallery Press, Loughcrew, Oldcastle, County Meath, Ireland from *The Reed Bed* (2001) · Seamus Heaney 'Mid-Term Break' from *Death of a Naturalist* by kind permission of Faber and Faber Ltd · John Hewitt 'For Roberta in the Garden' by kind permission of Blackstaff Press Ltd from *The Collected Poems of John Hewitt* (1991) · Douglas Hyde 'My Grief on the Sea' (from the Irish) reprinted with kind permission of Douglas Sealy · The two poems by Patrick Kavanagh are reprinted by kind permission of the Trustees of the Estate of the late Katherine B Kavanagh, through the Jonathan Williams Literary Agency · Thomas Kinsella 'She's the Blackberry-Flower' (from the Irish) from *Collected Poems* reprinted by kind permission of Carcanet Press Ltd · 'Ceasefire' from *Selected Poems* by Michael Longley published by Jonathan Cape. Used by permission of The Random House Group Limited · 'Ceasefire' by Michael Longley used by kind permission of Wake Forest University Press (US) · Louis MacNeice 'Autobiography' from *Collected Poems* published by Faber and Faber Ltd reprinted by kind permission of David Higham Associates Ltd · Derek Mahon 'An Image from Beckett' by kind permission of the author and The Gallery Press, Loughcrew, Oldcastle, County Meath, Ireland from *Collected Poems* (1999) · Aidan Carl

Mathews 'Minding Ruth' by kind permission of the author and The Gallery Press, Loughcrew, Oldcastle, County Meath, Ireland from *Minding Ruth* (1983) · Paula Meehan 'Would you Jump into my Grave as Quick?' by kind permission of the author and The Gallery Press, Loughcrew, Oldcastle, County Meath, Ireland from *Pillow Talk* (1994) · Máire Mhac an tSaoi 'Keep to Yourself Your Kisses' (from the Irish) reprinted by kind permission of Máire Mhac an tSaoi · John Montague 'All Legendary Obstacles' by kind permission of the author and The Gallery Press, Loughcrew, Oldcastle, County Meath, Ireland from *Collected Poems* (1995) · Paul Muldoon 'Holy Thursday' from *Why Brownlee Left* by kind permission of Faber and Faber Ltd · Richard Murphy 'Moonshine' by kind permission of the author and The Gallery Press, Loughcrew, Oldcastle, County Meath, Ireland from *Collected Poems* (2000) · Eiléan Ní Chuilleanáin 'That Summer' by kind permission of the author and The Gallery Press, Loughcrew, Oldcastle, County Meath, Ireland from *The Brazen Serpent* (1994) · Nuala Ní Dhomhnaill 'Primavera' and Medbh McGuckian 'Primavera' (from the Irish) by kind permission of the authors and The Gallery Press, Loughcrew, Oldcastle, County Meath, Ireland from *The Water Horse* (1999) · Julie O'Callaghan 'The Deal' from *No Can Do*, Bloodaxe Books, 2000 · Frank O'Connor 'On the Death of His Wife' (from the Irish) reprinted by kind permission of the Estate of Frank O'Connor · 'Lesser Deaths' from *The Weakness* by Bernard O'Donoghue published by Chatto & Windus. Used by Permission of The Random House Group Limited · 'Years After' is taken from *Exemplary Damages* by Dennis O'Driscoll published by Anvil Press Poetry in 2002 · Desmond O'Grady 'The Lass from Bally-na-Lee' (from the Irish) by kind permission of the author and The Gallery Press, Loughcrew, Oldcastle, County Meath, Ireland from *A Limerick Rake* (1978) · Sheila O'Hagan, 'Father' reprinted with kind permission of Sheila O'Hagan · Mary O'Malley 'Starting School' from *The Boning Hall* reprinted by kind permission of Carcanet Press Ltd (1993) · Frank Ormsby 'Helen' by kind permission of the author and The Gallery Press, Loughcrew, Oldcastle, County Meath, Ireland from *The Ghost Train* (1995) · Tom Paulin 'Traces' from *Selected Poems 1972–1990* by kind permission of Faber and Faber Ltd · W R Rodgers 'The Lovers' by kind permission of the author and The Gallery Press, Loughcrew, Oldcastle, County Meath, Ireland from *Poems* (1993) · James Simmons 'For Thomas Moore' by kind permission of the author and The Gallery Press, Loughcrew, Oldcastle, County Meath, Ireland from *Poems 1956–1986* (1986) · W B Yeats 'Politics' reprinted with permission of A P Watt Ltd on behalf of Michael B Yeats

INDEX OF FIRST LINES